Carving & Painting a
BLACK-CAPPED CHICKADEE
with Ernest Muehlmatt

Curtis J. Badger

STACKPOLE BOOKS

Published by
STACKPOLE BOOKS
5067 Ritter Road
Mechanicsburg, PA 17055

Printed in Hong Kong

10 9 8 7 6 5 4 3 2 1

First edition

Library of Congress Cataloging-in-Publication Data

Badger, Curtis J.
    Carving and painting a black-capped chickadee with Ernest
Muehlmatt / Curtis J. Badger.
      p.   cm.
    ISBN 0-8117-2423-9 (pb)
    1. Wood-carving.   2. Black-capped chickadee in art.   I. Title.
TT199.7.B332   1997
736'.4—dc20   96-41798
                                             CIP

Contents

CHAPTER ONE

Ernest Muehlmatt: Artist and Teacher

For more than twenty years, Ernie Muehlmatt has been one of the most respected wildfowl artists and teachers in America. As an artist, he has won the prestigious Ward World Championship Wildfowl Carving Competition three times, and his work is included in some of the leading public and private collections in the country. As a teacher, he has conducted workshops from coast to coast, launching dozens of beginning artists on careers of their own. His book *Songbird Carving with Ernest Muehlmatt* (Stackpole Books) is one of the best-selling instructional bird-carving books on the market.

Ernie began his career in wildlife art after spending twenty years in his family's florist business near Philadelphia, turning a lifelong interest in birds and a talent for art into a full-time career. "I enlisted in the army near the end of World War II and spent a year in Alaska and really enjoyed the birds and wildlife where I was stationed in the Aleutian Islands," he says. "I did a lot of bird-watching there and it built up my interest. When I got out I went to school at the Philadelphia College of Art for a year, then to the Advertising and Art Students League and graduated from there."

As a young man, Ernie had both a fascination for birds and formal training in art, but the two would not be combined for nearly twenty years. By the time Ernie graduated from art school his father had become ill and Ernie and his brother went to work managing the family flower and garden business in Marple Township. Ernie's artistic talents were put to use designing floral arrangements.

"We ran the business for twenty years and we both hated it," he says. "It got to the point when we were both around forty that we got fed up with it and decided to get out while we still had our sanity. It was just about at this time that I heard about the first Ward Foundation bird-carving exhibition in Salisbury, Maryland. I hadn't done any carving at the time, but I had thought about it, so I drove down to see what it was all about. I

1

remember driving down to Salisbury in a terrible rainstorm and almost turning around and going back home several times. But I got to the show and I was just floored. There were artists there like Arnold Melbye and Wendell Gilley, and I talked with them and marveled at their work, and it just so happened that the chairman of the show that year was Bob Dunn, whom I had gone to high school with. He had moved to Salisbury. So I went home and started carving, and the next fall I called Bob and asked him if he could get me in the show. I didn't really deserve to be there, but he got me in, and that started the whole thing."

Even in those early years, Ernie was focusing on songbirds, which today remain his specialty. "I did a lot of chickadees and sold them for three bucks," he says. "Then they went up to six, and then ten, then fifteen. Eventually I got to the point where I could make a living at carving."

The florist business closed, and Ernie converted the shop to a carving studio and classroom, where carvers could come for week-long seminars. The shop was closed last year when Ernie moved to the Eastern Shore of Maryland, where he now conducts his seminars.

Ernie's careers as artist and teacher have run along parallel tracks. After exhibiting at the Ward Foundation shows in the early 1970s his work became increasingly popular, and he was invited to exhibit at many shows around the country. A very patient and generous man, Ernie soon became regarded as an outstanding teacher who has no secrets when it comes to the technical aspects of carving and painting. Beginning bird carvers have found that a week spent with Ernie in a seminar can make them proficient carvers, thus shortening the learning curve considerably.

Ernie is one of the few wildfowl artists to have won the Ward World Championship in two different categories. A carving of woodcocks won in 1979 in miniatures, as did a least bittern in 1981. In 1984 Ernie won the $20,000 purchase award in decorative life-size wildfowl carvings with a masterful work depicting bobwhite quail, cactus, and a cattle skull. All three of these pieces are part of the permanent collection of the Ward Museum in Salisbury, Maryland.

In this book, Ernie carves and paints a chickadee, a bird he began his career with, selling it for a few dollars. His chickadees fetch somewhat more than that these days, but then, Ernie's talents as a carver and painter are considerably farther along than they were back then.

Rather than assembling parts carved separately, Ernie carves from a single block of wood, believing that the process is more sculptural. Thus, the chickadee, the branch on which it is perched, and the base are all made from a single block of tupelo. It is a fairly simple design and arrangement, with the S curve of the weathered branch the dominant feature of the composition. The colors, too, complement each other, with the rich browns and grays occurring not only in the bird, but in the branch and the base, which is painted to resemble granite.

This project offers beginning or intermediate carvers several valuable lessons, beginning with the overall composition of the work and the importance of working out the design on paper before committing it to wood. There is obviously the object lesson in how to carve a chickadee, but the bird is only part of the composition. The reader should consider the visual elements of the entire work, including textures, colors, design, and accuracy of detail. All of these are important, and in this project an outstanding artist, technician, and teacher demonstrates how they work together to create an impressive three-dimensional sculpture that includes a bird as its center of interest.

Ernie Muehlmatt at work in his studio.

3

Ernie's studio in Pennsylvania includes lots of natural light.

Ernie at work on an osprey carving.

Ernie applies head detail to a life-size carving of an osprey.

Ernie conducts a workshop at the Ward Museum in Salisbury, Maryland.

CHAPTER TWO

About the Chickadee

Chickadees are members of the family Paridae, which includes the tufted titmouse, a bird widely found throughout the eastern half of the United States; the plain titmouse of the Southwest; and the boreal chickadee of Canada and Alaska.

But if you mention chickadee to most people, the image it stirs is that of the friendly little bird with the black cap and bib, a regular visitor to backyard feeding stations. If you live in the northern United States or Canada, the bird cracking open those sunflower seeds in your feeder is probably the black-capped chickadee. South of the Mason-Dixon line, it would more likely be the Carolina chickadee.

The birds appear very similar and may hybridize where their ranges overlap. The main distinction is one of sound. The black-cap's call is a lower and slower version of the Carolina's "chick-a-dee-dee-dee."

Fortunately, we don't have to concern ourselves with calls and songs when carving and painting a wooden bird, so this project could easily be a Carolina or black-capped chickadee. The two major visual distinctions are these: The black-cap is slightly larger, and it has white edges on its wing coverts and secondary feathers. The bird Ernie will be carving and painting in this book is a black-capped chickadee, *Parus atricapillus,* not because he has anything against the South, but because he was living in Pennsylvania when this project was done and those are the birds that frequented his feeders.

If you want to do a Carolina version of the chickadee, make it a centimeter shorter and omit the white feather edges. With a little imagination and some good reference material, you could even turn the bird into a Mexican or mountain chickadee.

The chickadees, or more accurately the Paridae, constitute perhaps the most popular bird family in America. Most of us have had our winters warmed by the sight of these compact little birds at our feeders. They are friendly, gregarious, and can become almost tame. It's not that difficult to get a chickadee to take sunflower seeds from your hand.

According to John Terres's *Audubon Society Encyclopedia of North American Birds,* the name titmouse comes from a combination of Old Icelandic and Anglo-Saxon words. The former gives us *titr,* meaning something small, while mouse is a corruption of the word *mase,* Anglo-Saxon for a kind of bird. The name chickadee is derived from the bird's call.

Terres describes the chickadee as "having soft, thick plumage, mostly grays and browns, all have short and stout pointed bills, nostrils partly covered with bristles, short strong legs and feet, rounded wings each with ten primary feathers, with the outermost, or first, only half the length of the second." Male and female chickadees have similar plumage.

Chickadees are migratory within their range. They don't fly to the tropics in fall like warblers, vireos, and tanagers, but they do move southward after the nesting season. In winter they join family groups in loose bands that often include nuthatches, creepers, kinglets, and woodpeckers.

Chickadees feed on a combination of plants and insects. Their diet includes moths, caterpillars, ants, insect eggs, spiders, and beetles. Those who have bird feeders can attest to the chickadee's affinity for black oil sunflower seeds, suet, and various small grains. In the wild, chickadees will feed on the seeds of conifers and wild berries.

Chickadees are cavity nesters and in spring seek out rotting stumps, knotholes, and abandoned woodpecker nests. I recently found a pair nesting in a small space behind a thick poison-ivy vine as it wound around a sweet-gum tree.

According to Terres, both sexes excavate the nest site, and the female lines it with plant fibers, hairs, wool, mosses, feathers, and insect cocoons. Six to eight eggs are laid from April to July, and incubation, which is done by both parents, takes eleven to thirteen days. The young leave the nest when they are fourteen to eighteen days old.

The body length of the black-capped chickadee is about 13 centimeters, or $5^{1/4}$ inches. The Carolina chickadee is a centimeter shorter. The dimensions of the bird Ernie is carving in this project differ somewhat because it is depicted in a resting posture, perched on a weathered tree branch. It is about 10 centimeters from head to tail.

The chickadee's gregarious personality, curiosity, and friendliness toward humans have made it one of our favorite birds for many years. Indeed, it is the state bird of Maine and Massachusetts. Even professional ornithologists are sometimes swayed from scientific objectivity and describe the chickadee in anthropomorphic terms. Chester A. Reed, the noted ornithologist and author of a popular series of bird guides in the early 1900s, described the chickadee as "one of the most popular birds that we have, owing to their uniform good nature, even in the coldest weather, and their confiding disposition."

The chickadee may or may not have a "confiding disposition," but it definitely is a handsome, dapper little bird. With world champion artist Ernie Muehlmatt leading the way, I hope you will enjoy carving and painting it.

Black-capped chickadee by Ernie Muehlmatt.

11

CHAPTER THREE

Getting Started

Ernie uses high-speed grinders with a variety of bits to carve the bird, and in the field of decorative, realistic bird carving, these tools are invaluable. The bird could be carved with knives, but high-speed grinders, with bits that come in myriad shapes and sizes, are almost a necessity for this type of carving.

Ernie also uses a burning pen, or pyrographic tool, for adding fine feather detail such as barbs and quills. This, too, is a necessity in realistic, highly detailed bird carving.

A band saw is used to rough out the general shape of the carving, and if you don't have one, try to cultivate a friendship with someone who does. Failing that, you could rough out the bird with a coping saw or take the block of wood to a woodworking shop and ask them to do the work for you.

When using any power tool, be sure to read and understand the safety instructions that came with it. Wear protective eyeglasses when recommended by manufacturers, and use some type of dust filtering system when using grinders. Ernie has a dust removal system of his own design, and you'll read more about that later.

One of the most important non-tools you will need is reference material. This could be photographs, videotapes, or even mounted birds or study skins. Keep in mind that songbirds are protected by law, and it's illegal to possess carcasses without a permit. Many museums and natural history organizations have collections of mounted birds and skins and will often provide access to artists.

Another important addition to your work table is a sketch pad and pencil. Ernie always designs his carving on paper before committing it to wood, and this is especially important when doing the entire piece—bird, base, and branch—from a single block of wood. The time you spend thinking about design and composition in the planning stages will save you much anguish later.

Side view of the chickadee, to scale.
This sketch can be photocopied and
used as a pattern, or you could work
out a composition of your own. See
page 16 for specific dimensions.

The front view, also to scale. The weathered branch is depicted with roots spreading over a granite rock, and Ernie has included some of that detail in the sketch as he works out the composition on paper.

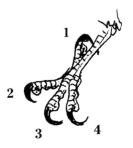

A side view of the head with lines showing the margins of the black cap. The bill is 7mm long.

The left foot is visible in this carving; only the toes of the right foot will show. The lengths of the toes is as follows: #1—10mm; #2—7mm; #3—10mm; #4—8mm. The tarsus is 15mm in length. Toe #1 has one bone and no joints; #2 has two bones and one joint; #3 has three bones and two joints, and #4 has four bones and three joints. There will be more on this as the carving progresses.

Front view of the head, with lines showing the black bib.

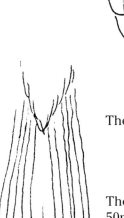

The left wing showing coverts and primary and secondary feathers. The length of the wing is approximately 60mm.

The right wing.

The tail is approximately 50mm long.

BASIC TOOLS AND SUPPLIES

Here is a list of the basic tools and supplies you'll need for carving and painting the chickadee:

- Photos of chickadees and/or study skins for reference material
- A sketch pad and pencil
- A block of tupelo or comparable carving stock approximately 5 x 8 x 9 inches
- Two 5mm dark brown glass eyes
- Water soluble epoxy putty for mounting the eyes
- Access to a band saw
- A high-speed grinding tool, with a minimum of one stump cutter and three sizes (1mm to 5mm) of diamond cutters
- Stone bits for texturing
- A pyrographic instrument for burning feather detail
- Acrylic tube paints in ultramarine blue, burnt umber, and raw sienna, plus gesso. Speedball brand warm black for the head

This list represents a bare minimum. As you go along, you will find that other tools and supplies—a hair dryer for quickly drying paint, for example—can become indispensable.

Ernie begins the project by making a sketch of the bird, the branch on which it is perched, and the base. The carving will be made from a single piece of tupelo gum, so it's important to work out the composition now. He designs this piece based on the S curve; the shape of the branch will determine the overall composition of the piece. You can use the diagram provided, or you can work out a composition of your own.

Ernie's sketch on paper is cut out, and the outline is traced onto the block of tupelo, which then goes to the band saw. And thus we begin.

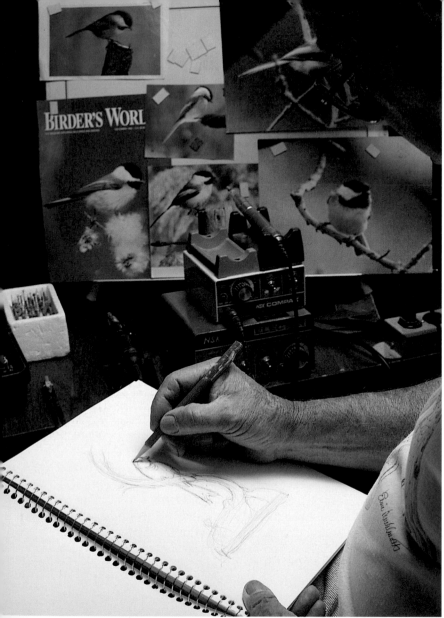

Ernie begins the project on the sketch pad, using various photographs as reference material. Measurements taken from study skins provide anatomical accuracy. A federal permit is required to collect study skins or taxidermy mounts, but natural history museums and nature centers will often allow artists access to their collections.

"Start with any kind of line," Ernie advises. "You can use a circle, a C shape, or, as in this case, an S curve. This provides the overall composition of the piece, the visual interest. Once you come up with a pleasing composition, you add the bird."

It's important to spend some time with the sketch, working out the composition you want. This serves as the blueprint of the carving, so an unsuccessful sketch is unlikely to lead to a pleasing three-dimensional carving, no matter how much time you spend carving and painting the bird.

"You need to develop some ability to visualize, to think about how a carving depicted in a two-dimensional sketch will look in three dimensions," says Ernie. "You also need some knowledge of bird design, bird anatomy, to create a realistic and believable carving."

When Ernie is satisfied with the sketch, he cuts it out. The outline will be used as a pattern.

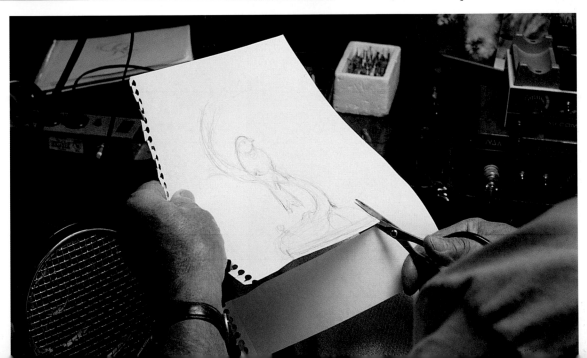

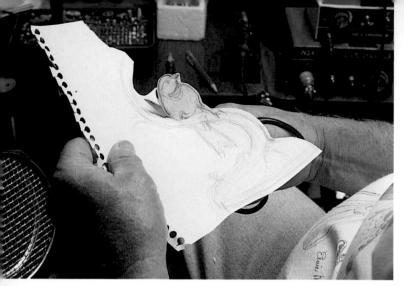

The sketch actually serves two functions. It becomes a pattern for cutting out the tupelo, but it contains a great deal more detail than required for a pattern. In the sketch, Ernie works out many factors of the composition, such as how the roots will lie over the rock.

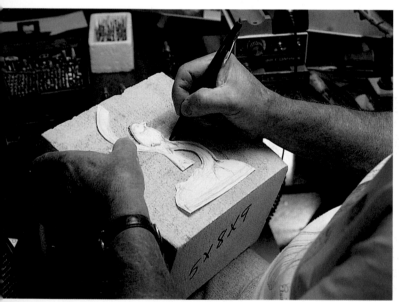

Ernie traces the front outline onto a block of tupelo. The outline is situated so areas where the wood will be thin, such as the tail, go with the direction of the grain. This adds strength to these areas.

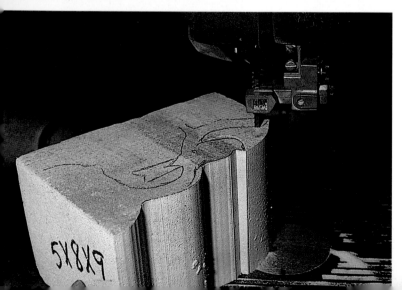

The outline is cut out on the band saw. Be sure to follow the manufacturer's safety instructions when using power tools. Have a local cabinet shop cut the bird out for you if you do not have a band saw.

The front outline is nearly complete. The band saw makes the job quick and easy. Smaller power tools or a hand saw could be used, however.

With the front outline cut, Ernie begins sketching the side view onto the wood.

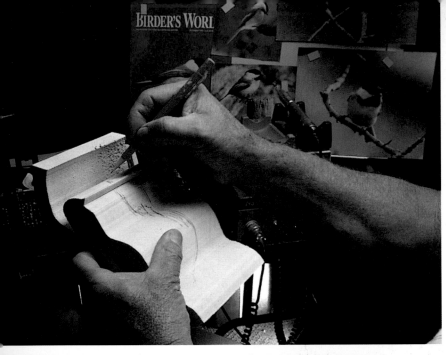

Ernie freehands the side view; you can use the pattern on page 14. The pattern is drawn to scale, so simply photocopy it and sketch the outline onto the wood.

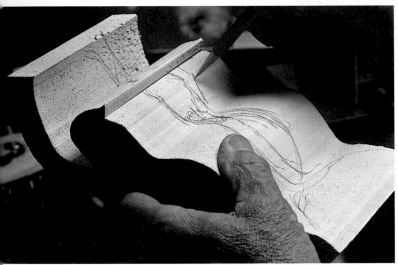

"The advantage of carving from one piece of wood is the freedom it provides," says Ernie. "I can sit down with a block of wood and do just about anything I can imagine. I don't have to worry about adding on parts, finding feet that fit with the composition, and making an appropriate base and mount for the bird. If you're doing a painting, you don't paint different sections separately and then paste them onto the canvas; you approach the work as a whole."

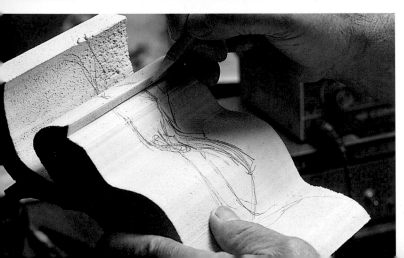

Ernie prefers working with tupelo because it is nearly grainless, sapless, very strong, and light in weight. Balsa wood with strength is a good description.

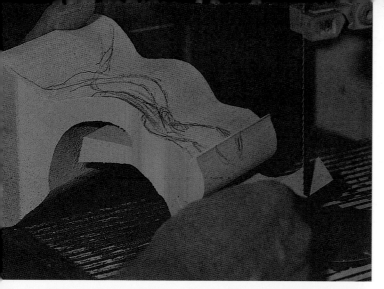

The side profile is cut out on the band saw, following the pencil lines that Ernie sketched onto the wood. Again, if you are not experienced in using a band saw, have the piece cut out for you at a woodworking shop.

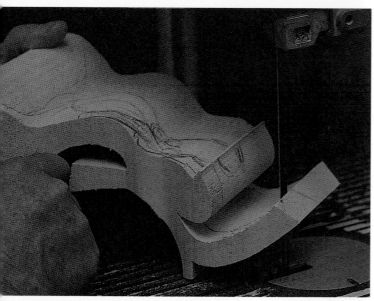

As the side profile is cut, a rough three-dimensional figure begins to take shape. Ernie frequently sketches detail on the carving as part of his planning process.

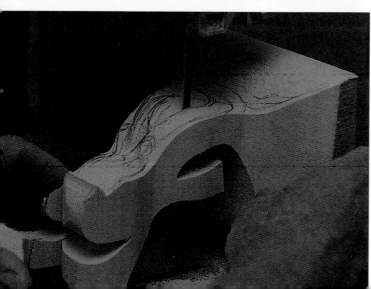

Ernie removes all the wood he can with the band saw, as this is much quicker than using grinding tools. Safety is paramount, however, so unless you are very experienced with this tool, have a professional do it for you.

CHAPTER FOUR

Roughing Out the Head

At this point in the carving process, Ernie has cut out the three-dimensional figure on the band saw and is ready to rough out the shape, beginning with the bill and head. If you had your carving cut out for you at a woodworking shop, you would be at this stage—ready to go to work with the high-speed grinder in your own shop.

As you rough out the carving, refer often to the diagrams and dimensions provided in chapter 3. They are like a road map, guiding you on your way. It would be a good idea to make photocopies and have them on your work table at all times.

Ernie uses a high-speed grinder with a variety of cutting bits for roughing out. Many makes and models of grinders are on the market, ranging in price from $100 or less and upward. The more expensive models tend to turn at greater RPMs and have more torque. If you're in the market for a grinder, attend a carving show and visit the various retailers, or go to a carving supplies shop. Most will allow you to try the tool before purchasing.

For roughing out, Ernie's favorite tool is a sharp barrel-shaped bit called a stump cutter, which can remove a lot of wood in a short period of time.

Another very important "tool" in your shop should be some sort of dust removal system. Using a high-speed grinder on tupelo generates a lot of fine dust, which is extremely harmful to the respiratory system. As with high-speed grinders, a wide variety of dust removal systems are on the market. Some carvers use simple methods such as mounting a vacuum cleaner nozzle on the work area; others use sophisticated ventilation systems that remove dust to the outside.

Ernie has designed a system of his own called the Dust Devil. A quiet, powerful fan pulls airborne dust particles into a cloth bag. The fan is mounted on a tripod and can be adjusted to various heights or moved to different locations. For information on the Dust Devil, write Ernie at Old Marple Road, Springfield, PA 19046, or call 1-800-946-2944.

25

As he begins roughing out the carving, Ernie starts with the bill and the head, first drawing a centerline that will determine the angle of the bill and head. "It all begins with the bill," he says. "You begin there, go to the head, then the nape, the back, the tail. Carving is a matter of going from one bird part to the next. Once you determine the location of the bill, that dictates the position of the head, the eyes, and everything else. You begin with the bill and go from there."

With the carving cut out on the band saw, Ernie uses the grinding tool to refine the shape. Many makes and models of high-speed grinders are on the market, beginning at about $100.

High-speed grinders can be fitted with a wide variety of bits. This one is called a stump cutter and can remove wood quickly. The better quality grinders have higher torque and turn at greater RPMs than less expensive models.

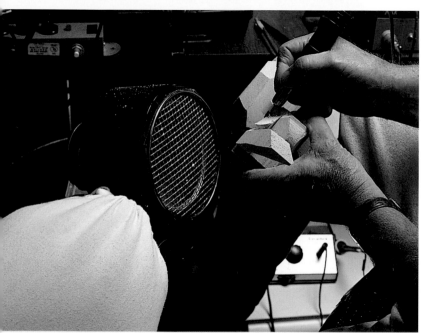

Some method of dust removal must be used with a high-speed grinder. This system, which makes use of a cage fan and cloth bag, was designed by Ernie and is called the Dust Devil. Airborne dust is harmful to the respiratory system, so a dust removal system is important.

A stump cutter, a thick cylinder with sharp rasplike teeth, can make the shavings fly. Stump cutters also come in other shapes, such as tapered cylinders and balls. Use the one that is most efficient for the job.

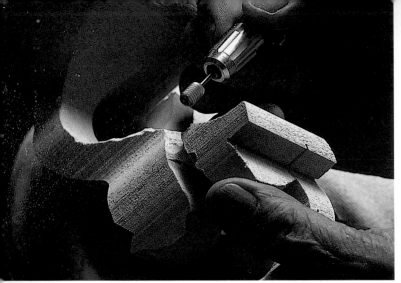

The stump cutter removes a lot of wood in a short time yet provides reasonable accuracy and control. Ernie uses it for everything from roughing out to more intricate carving.

What Ernie is doing at this stage is simply removing wood he could not reach with the band saw. This is the front profile of the chickadee.

Before going any farther, Ernie draws a centerline and sketches the top profile of the chickadee's head. The centerline also represents the center of the bill, and consequently the angle at which the head is turned.

He uses the stump cutter to remove wood down to the shoulder level. Refer to the dimensions on page 16 for head and bill measurements. Measure carefully, and be sure not to remove too much wood.

The centerline is the carver's most valuable reference and should remain on the wood throughout the carving process. Ernie measures from the centerline to determine the width of the head, which is sketched in pencil.

The stump cutter is used to round off edges and create contours, as the head of the bird gradually takes shape. The bill should be approximately 7mm long.

A 4mm diamond cutter is used to relieve the side profile. The centerline is kept as a reference point. "I do a lot of drawing on the bird as I carve," says Ernie. "It helps me visualize what I want to do."

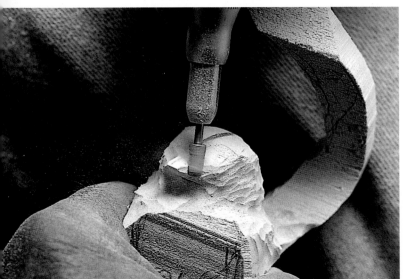

The diamond cutter is used to rough out the side profile of the bill. The bill is the first specific element of the carving and will determine where other features will go. "Begin with the bill and the rest of the head will follow," says Ernie.

The bill determines the angle of the head, the location of the eyes, and the facial contour. "Selecting the location of the bill is arbitrary," says Ernie, "but once you make that decision, it determines many other things. Fastened to that bill, of course, is the head, so you begin with the bill and follow it one step at a time with other parts."

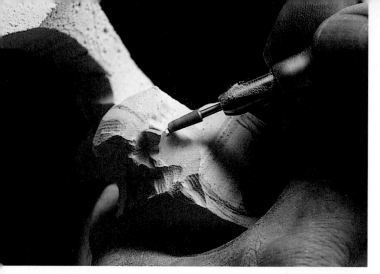

A smaller diamond cutter is used to refine the shape of the bill. Ernie has now roughed out the top and side profiles. Measure frequently and consult reference material to ensure accuracy.

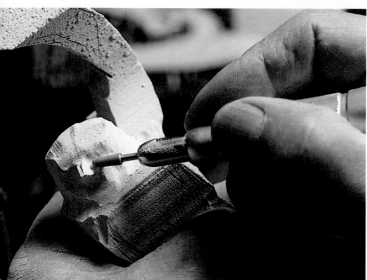

The bill will determine placement of the eyes, the cheeks, and other facial detail. "It all starts with the bill, then it goes to the head, the cape, the wings, the chest, the tail. It begins here and all falls into place," says Ernie.

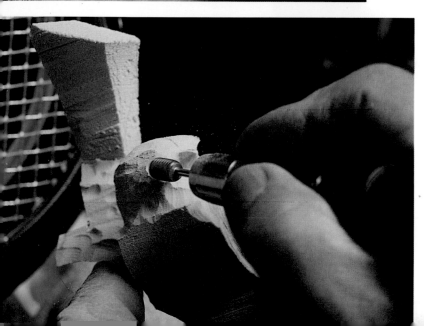

The next step is to rough out the head, cutting it down to its final dimensions. (Refer to the front and side profiles in chapter 3 for dimensions.) Ernie goes back to the stump cutter for this.

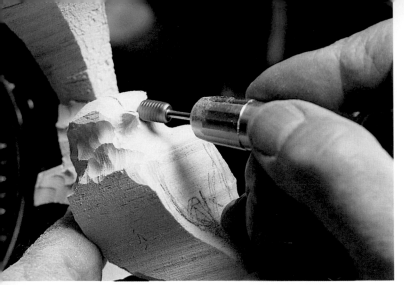

Once the head is cut down to proper dimensions, Ernie uses the stump cutter to carve eye channels on either side. These grooves must be symmetrical, so sketch the locations in pencil before carving.

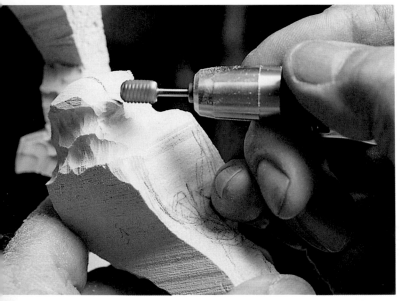

Ernie holds the bird so he can look at it head-on, then removes the same amount of wood from either side, ensuring that the head will be symmetrical. The grooves should be of the same depth and at the same distance from the crown of the head.

The stump cutter is used to carve a shallow groove on a line directly behind the bill. This groove determines the position of the eye, and, again, the two must be symmetrical.

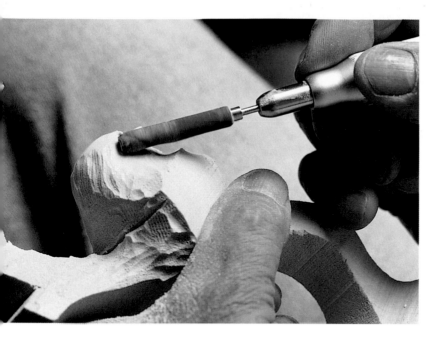

Once the groove is cut, Ernie uses a mandrel with sandpaper to smooth the wood. This will allow him to sketch in the eye position and to begin adding detail to the carving.

CHAPTER FIVE

The Eyes, the Bill, and a Hint of Feathers

The head has been roughed out, the bill carved, and the dimensions are as they will be in the final carving. The next step is to determine where the eyes will go and to drill holes to accept two 5mm glass eyes.

As demonstrated in chapter 4, the entire carving begins with the bill, which determines the angle at which the head is set, the location of the eyes, and indeed all the other elements of the carving.

Ernie locates the eyes by consulting his reference material—photographs, study skins, and patterns—and he uses dividers to make sure the eyes are the same distance from the tip of the bill. This step is vital in preserving symmetry.

Once the location of the eyes is determined, Ernie carefully drills the holes with a diamond cutter on his high-speed grinder. The two 5mm glass eyes are trial-fitted at this point but are not permanently mounted. The reason Ernie locates the eyes and drills the holes now is that the eyes are the next step in the carving process. Just as the position of the bill determined the location of the eyes, the position of the eyes determines how various facial details will be carved.

Once the eye holes are drilled, Ernie will begin to add feather detail to the head. The first step in this process is to cut various grooves and then to round off their edges. This is the initial phase in the texturing process, a trompe l'oeil technique intended to transform a hard block of wood into a downy patch of feathers.

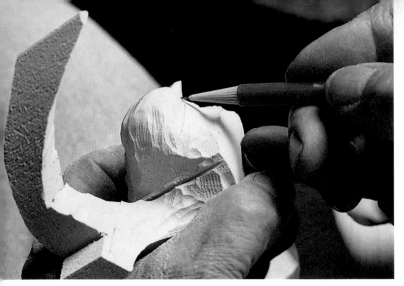

Ernie extends the line separating the upper and lower bill along the head. This will help locate the eyes, which lie along this line. When sketching these lines, check frequently to be sure they are symmetrical.

Ernie sketches the right eye first, placing it just above the line drawn in step one. Ernie does the right eye first because when he installs the left eye, he will be able to see the right one as he works with the face of the bird toward him. This makes it easier to have the eyes symmetrical.

To ensure correct placement of the left eye, Ernie looks at the carving from the front and sketches the eye on the same plane as the right one. It's important not to have one eye higher or lower than the other.

Dividers are used to make sure the eyes are the same distance from the tip of the bill. Ernie also checks the location visually by looking from the top of the head.

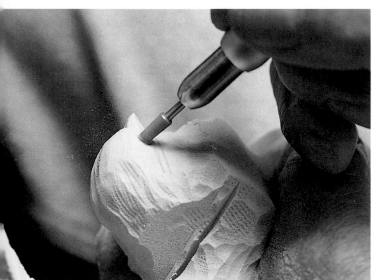

A 2mm diamond bullet is used to drill the holes for the eyes, and Ernie checks the fit occasionally as the hole is being drilled and enlarged. The glass eyes are 5mm in diameter, and the holes are slowly enlarged to that dimension.

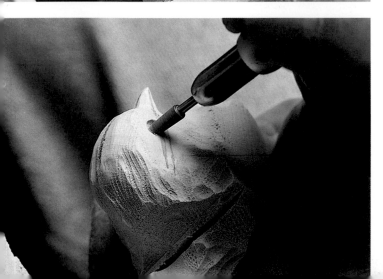

A smaller cutter is used because it gives Ernie more control in making small adjustments in the location of the eyes. If he used a 5mm cutter, the first cut would be the last, leaving no room for error.

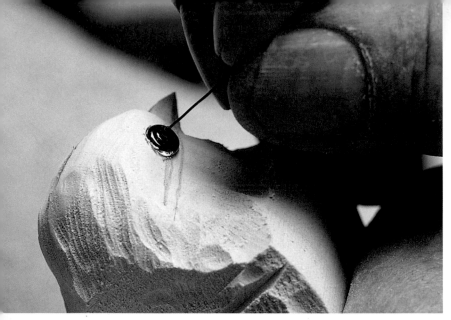

The glass eye is 5mm in diameter and approximately 3mm deep. Ernie tries for a snug fit. The hole should be deep enough that the surface of the eye is flush with the surface of the wood when it is pushed all the way in.

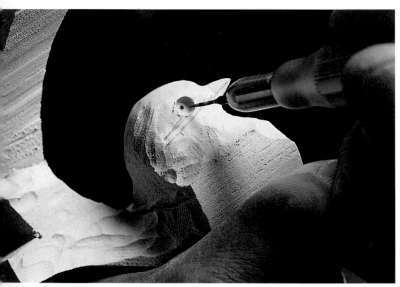

A small drill is used to put a hole in the center of each eye socket. This hole will accept the mounting wire attached to the glass eye. The eyes are attached to each other by the wire; Ernie snips them off, leaving about 1/2 inch of wire. Later, Ernie will mount the eyes using a two-part epoxy to ensure a permanent seal.

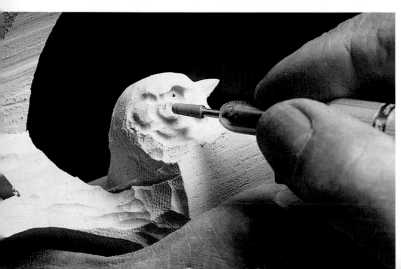

With the eye sockets installed, Ernie is ready to add preliminary feather detail to the head. He uses the same 2mm diamond bullet he used to carve the eye socket. The edge of the cutter is used to carve lines that replicate feather flow.

Ernie cuts a series of shallow grooves on the face of the chickadee. These represent the various muscle groups that underlie the feathers and skin: the auricular patch covering the ear; the malar track at the base of the bill, which includes the muscle that controls the lower bill; and another bump at the back of the head Ernie calls the "Bumpus Muehlmatt."

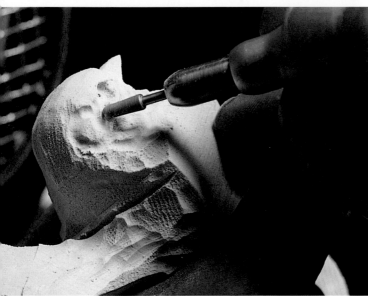

These grooves are carved as shown, and then the edges are smoothed out, with the cutter moving in the direction of the feather flow. These subtle bumps will add to the illusion of softness.

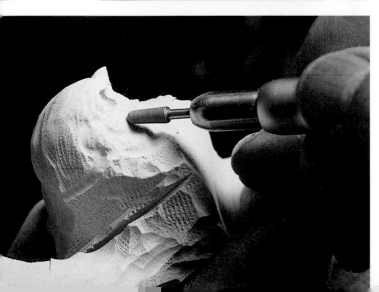

The goal here is to carve slight bumps and irregularities that represent muscle groups covered by feathers. It's important to keep the grooves shallow and to round off the edges of the grooves, making the effect as subtle as possible.

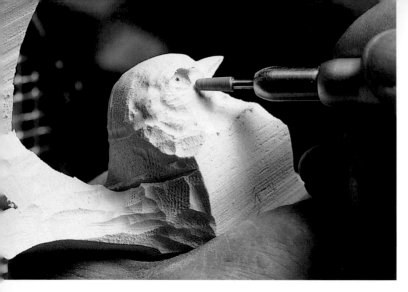

Ernie carves a slight rim under the eye, representing the eyelid. Further detail will be added after the 5mm glass eye has been inserted.

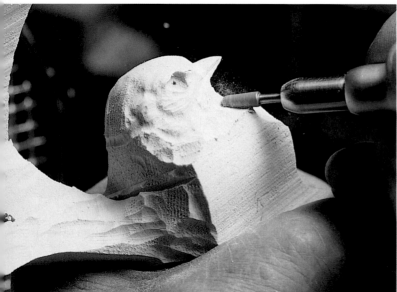

The neck area is reduced slightly to further define the position of the head. Again, Ernie works progressively from the bill, to the eyes, to the face, to the neck.

The same texturing technique is performed on the other side of the head, and now Ernie is ready to carve the wings. Before carving, be sure you have reference material handy, and refer to the dimensions on page 16.

CHAPTER SIX

Carving the Wings

Good reference material is very important when carving the wings. You need to become very familiar with the layout of the wings; you need to know what the major groups of feathers are, where they are located, and how the individual feathers are shaped. Nothing is quite as helpful as having a study skin, a dried carcass you can hold and manipulate. This, coupled with a good basic text on avian anatomy and flight, will give you a quick education in the function of wings and how they lie when the bird is at rest.

Ernie begins carving the wings by first rounding out the body and then sketching and drawing the various feather groups: the primary feathers, the secondaries, and the coverts. It's important at this point to decide how the feathers and feather groups will lie. For example, Ernie has decided that the tips of the primary feathers will not overlap, and he will sketch them this way after the body has been rounded out.

Before going any farther with the carving, this is the type of decision you also will need to make. Study the layout of the wing feathers, consult photographs and other reference materials, and make some sketches on paper of how you want your chickadee to look, paying special attention at this point to the wings.

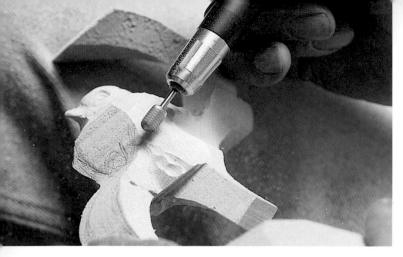

At this stage, the only part of the carving that has been reduced to finished dimensions is the head. Before carving the wings, Ernie must first round off the shape and carve the body down to the proper thickness. He does this with the stump cutter, beginning at the neck and working downward.

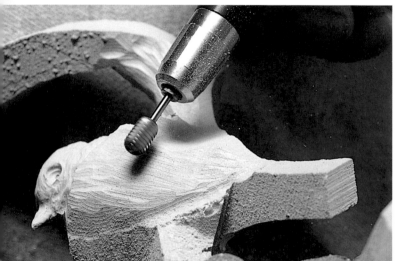

The cutter is used so that the texture lines approximate the direction of the flow of feathers. Refer to the dimensions on page 16 when roughing in the wings.

The back is roughed out, separating the bird from the branch on which it is perched.

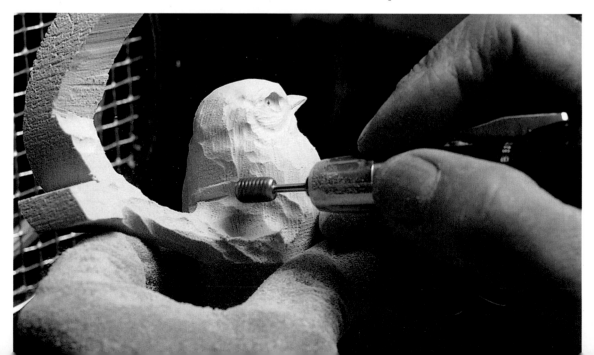

The bird is beginning to take shape now. Ernie uses study skins and other reference material to determine the proper dimensions, which are given in the pattern in chapter 3.

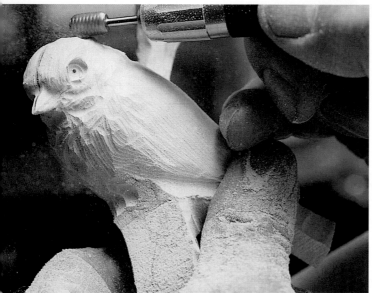

The back of the head and nape are reduced to size, and the area where the neck meets the body is defined. "It is often helpful to sketch some of these areas in pencil before carving," says Ernie.

With the body of the bird roughed out and reduced to finished dimensions, Ernie is ready to carve the wings. He uses a study skin to determine the overall length, which is approximately 60mm. He switches to the 2mm bullet to carve a groove separating the wings from the back.

At this stage, it's important to decide where the major feather groups—primaries, secondaries, coverts—will fall. Ernie sketches them in with a pencil.

A study skin is used to determine feather length and shape. A federal permit is needed to possess songbird skins, but many natural history museums will allow artists to use specimens in their collections.

The locations of the three major groups of wing feathers are sketched in pencil, and Ernie is ready to carve them with the 2mm bullet. From the top of the wing are the upper wing coverts, the secondaries, and the primaries.

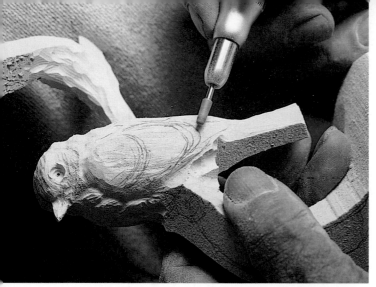

The bullet will be used to carve a groove along the pencil lines, delineating each feather group. Study photographs and taxidermy mounts, and be sure you understand the placement of different feather groups.

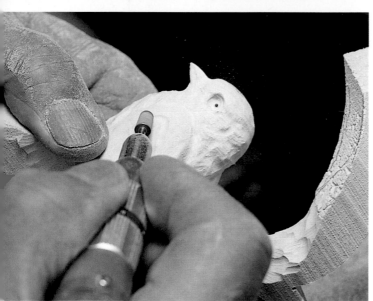

Ernie begins at the top of the wing carving a shallow groove that will represent the edge of the coverts. Most good field guides to birds have diagrams of the various flight feathers. Consult these before and during carving.

It's important to understand how the wings lie when the bird is at rest, and this sketch shows the approximate location of the major wing bones. The wing is similar to the human arm in that it has an upper arm, a forearm, a wrist, and fingers.

The feathers of the three major groups are drawn and will be defined with the burning pen once Ernie is satisfied with the placement and shape. Ten secondary feathers are attached to the forearm. The primaries are attached to what corresponds to the finger bones.

Ernie uses an offset burning tip designed by fellow bird artist Bob Guge to add feather detail. "Rather than carving each feather, you kind of iron them in with this. You can also do quills with it," says Ernie.

The burning pen is used to carve a shallow groove along each sketched line, delineating each feather. The hot tip of the pyrographic tool compresses the wood fibers, creating a fine, soft line.

Ernie burns a quill onto a secondary feather. Quills are carved by burning two parallel lines close to each other. The resultant ridge between the lines represents the quill.

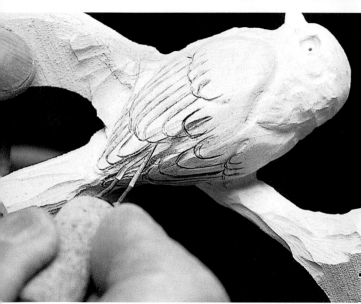

The outlines of the flight feathers are now carved. Later, Ernie will add texture to them using the burning pen and a small stone bit in his high-speed grinder. But for now, he wants to finish roughing out the carving, which means shaping the area where the feet join the branch on which the bird is perched.

CHAPTER SEVEN

Carving the Feet and Legs

One of the advantages of carving from a single block of wood is the freedom it gives you to make decisions as you go along. That point is certainly valid when carving the feet and legs. At this point, what Ernie has is a bird body fastened to a piece of wood about 1 inch square. Somewhere in that inch square are two legs, two feet, and a portion of weathered branch to which they are fastened. Ernie's next step is to determine where those legs and feet should be located and then to carve them.

The process is made a little easier for you, thanks to the patterns included in this book. Ernie based the design on sketches he made after looking at numerous photos of chickadees perched on weathered branches. Even though you have a pattern to go by, you might want to make sketches of your own. It's perfectly all right to alter the pattern included here, so use your imagination if you would like. Keep in mind, though, that this is a realistic carving, so consult reference material to determine size, shape, and anatomical accuracy. On the other hand, if a three-legged chickadee is your artistic vision . . .

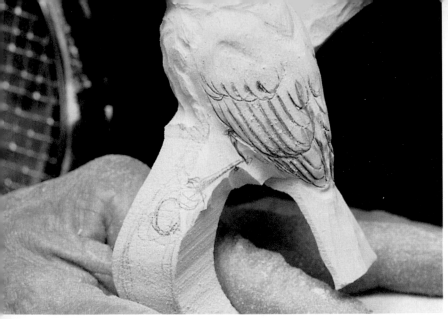

The number two lead pencil is one of Ernie's most frequently used tools. He sketches on the carving very often, and the pencil is indispensable for planning important details such as the location of the legs and feet. Here he makes a preliminary sketch showing the left leg and toes.

The legs should be midway beneath the bird, when viewed from the side, to provide the correct center of balance, and Ernie keeps this in mind when laying out the left leg. Be sure that the carving as a whole, and the bird itself, appear balanced.

Using various photographs as reference, Ernie sketches in the upper leg, knee, lower leg, and foot. The left leg and foot are visible in this carving, with the foot grasping the branch. The right leg, which is beneath the bird, will not be visible; only a part of the foot will show. (See pattern on page 16.)

Ernie uses the 2mm diamond bullet to remove wood and begin shaping the leg and foot. Begin carving only after you are sure your sketched detail is accurate.

Wood is removed from both sides of the leg bone, following the pencil sketch Ernie made earlier. Be sure to measure carefully to ensure that the dimensions are correct.

In making a one-piece carving, the process of defining the legs and feet also includes carving the mount, the branch on which the bird is resting. Ernie rounds this off and begins the preliminary shaping of it.

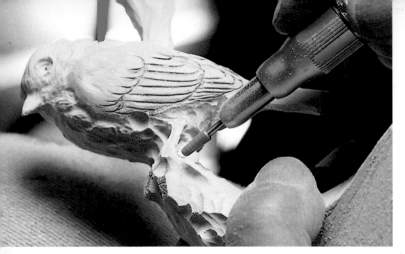

He undercuts the leg, separating it from the body. Be careful not to remove too much wood in this step.

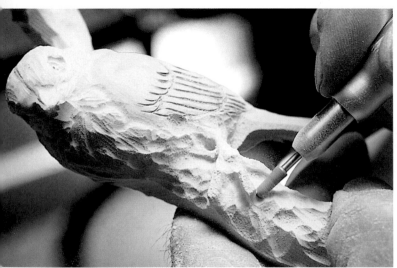

Ernie begins carving the foot, still using the 2mm bullet and following the pencil sketch he made earlier. The foot is composed of the heel and four toes. See the pattern for lengths of the leg and four toes.

With the toes roughed out, Ernie begins carving the claws, switching to a smaller 1mm bullet to undercut each claw, separating them from the branch.

The claws are undercut and rounded with the small bullet. See the drawings on page 16 for proper dimensions.

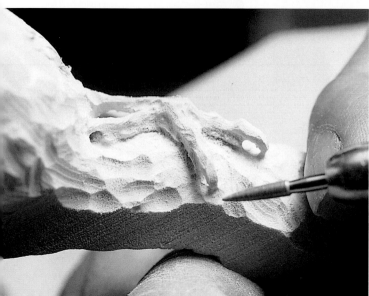

Ernie carves the joints in each toe by making a depression where the bones are located; the adjacent raised area represents the joint.

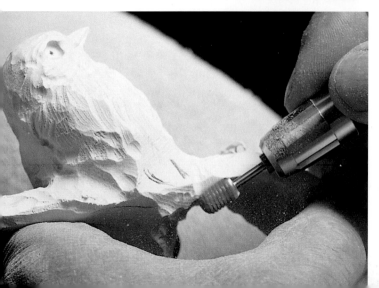

The right leg is under the bird and is not visible, but the toes will show where they are wrapped around the branch. Ernie sketches the location and removes wood around what will be the toes.

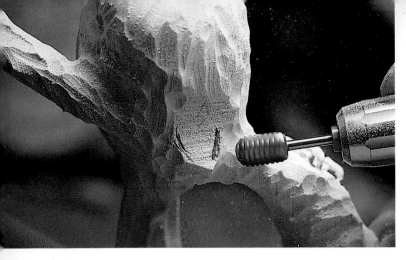

The right foot is under the center of the body. Ernie uses the stump cutter to rough it out and to further round off the weathered branch.

As he did on the left foot, Ernie uses the 1mm bullet to refine the shape of the toes on the right foot.

Both feet are now roughed out, along with the head, bill, and wings. Before adding fine detail to the bird, Ernie wants to refine the shape of the base.

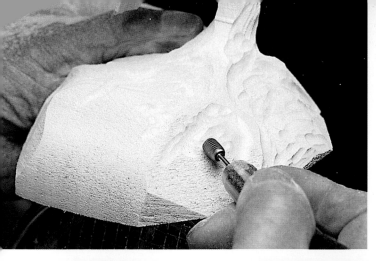

With a one-piece carving, it's helpful to work on it in its entirety, bringing all the elements together simultaneously. Ernie has decided to make the base a granite rock over which have grown the roots of a weathered tree. A patch of moss will be added for additional texture, color, and visual interest.

Ernie uses a stump cutter to shape the rock and define the roots, which spread at random over the rock. Accuracy is not all that important in this part of the process. Use your imagination and come up with interesting shapes and textures.

The roots are carved at random, but it's a good idea to do a rough sketch. "You really can't go wrong," says Ernie. "You'll always be able to find something in nature that resembles what you're doing. You could leave the rock smooth, giving the illusion of a very hard rock. But I like the weathered look with the facets and pimples. It goes well with the weathered wood."

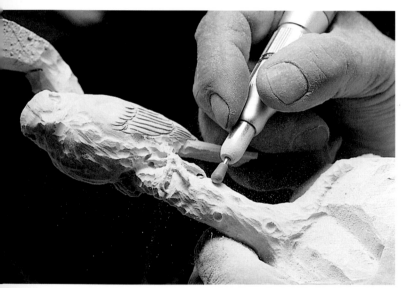

A carbide tip with a flat end is used to make facets in the rock, and then a bullet tip is used to make little pimples. The edge of the carbide tip is used to carve fine lines.

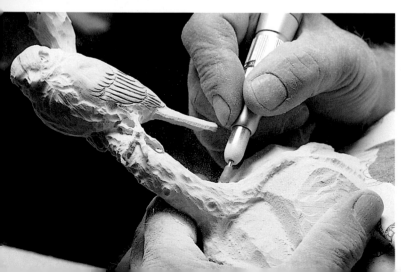

"You can add pock marks where a limb might have broken off, or you can make little elongated canoe shapes where the wood grew around a twig," says Ernie. "It's a dead gray stick with the bark worn off. You can do virtually anything you want."

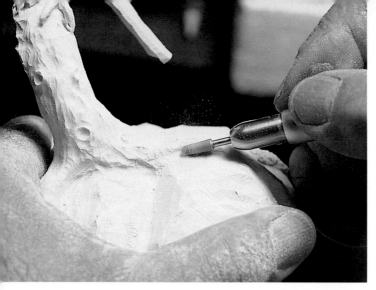

Ernie uses a combination of the flat cylinder and this rounded stone for most of the detail, then goes to a sharp point for tight places such as around the bird's feet.

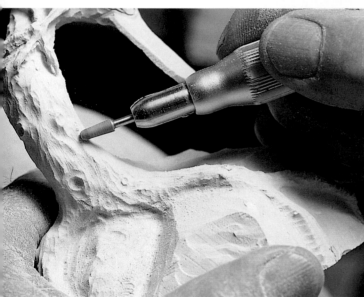

"You can do anything your imagination comes up with, or you can go outside, find a stick, and try to replicate it," Ernie says. "Once you come up with a good composition, you can do what you want with the details."

CHAPTER EIGHT

Adding Detail and Texture

The carving is now ready for fine-tuning. All the dimensional aspects are completed. That is, the bird has been carved to its true and final dimensions. The wings are of the correct length, and the flight feathers are carved. The head and face area is done, and the feet are carved. Now comes the fun part.

This is a realistic, lifelike carving, and over the past thirty years or so, Ernie has developed numerous tools and techniques to transform a block of tupelo gum from a Louisiana swamp into what appears to be a soft and fragile bird that might at any time take flight.

What we have at this point is a bird that is still emphatically wooden. These next steps will begin the artist's alchemy that will gradually transform wood into feathers, rock, and even moss. In this chapter Ernie will add detail to the feet, carve and shape the tail, insert the eyes, and begin adding feather detail.

He also will continue work on the base and tree branch. It's important when carving from one piece of wood to have all the elements of the carving progress simultaneously. The temptation is to first carve the bird and then worry about finding a suitable base on which to display it. But with Ernie's technique the rocky base, the branch, and the bird are all equal partners in a visual composition. So work on the base proceeds as does work on the bird.

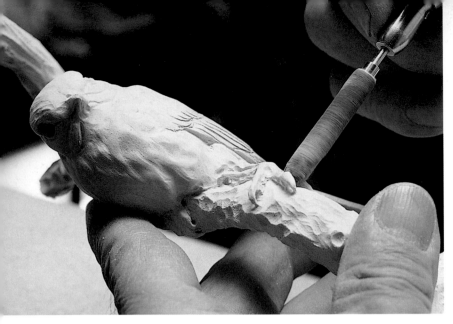

Prior to detailing the feet, Ernie lightly sands them with fine sandpaper mounted in a mandrel. This smoothes the surface and makes it easier to carve the fine detail that will come next.

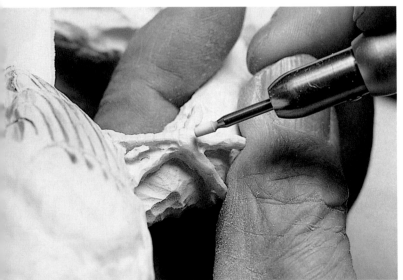

The upper part of the foot is scudulated—it has scales—while the lower area is reticulated, or pimpled. Ernie carves the scales with this small stone. Practice on a piece of smooth scrap tupelo before carving detail on the bird.

The pads of the feet are reticulated, and to add these small circles Ernie uses a small bit that has a concave point, which produces a slight cup shape.

The small circles are carved in a random manner, placed tightly together and sometimes overlapping. This bit is available at carving supply stores.

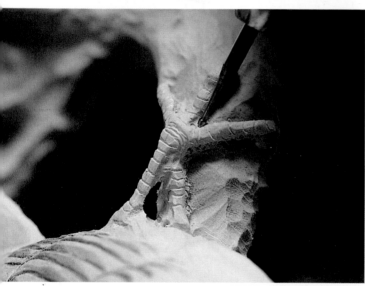

The foot is now textured, with scales on the top and reticulation on the pads. Ernie also adds scales to the right foot.

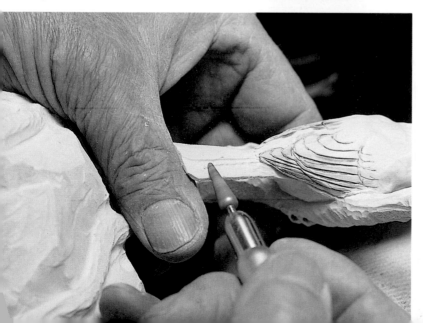

The last major feather group to be carved and textured is the tail. Ernie uses a tapered cylinder designed by bird artist Greg Woodard of Utah.

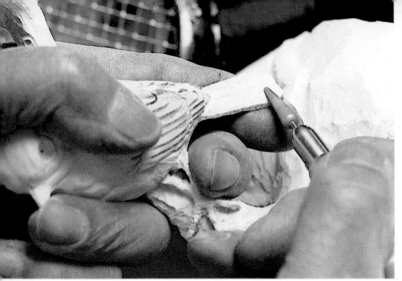

The tail feathers are carved with a slight curve, with the outside edges somewhat lower than the center. Refer to the dimensions on page 16 to ensure accuracy when carving these feathers.

The area under the tail is slightly concave. The tapered cylinder is handy for getting this shape. Again, good reference material is important in laying out and carving this area.

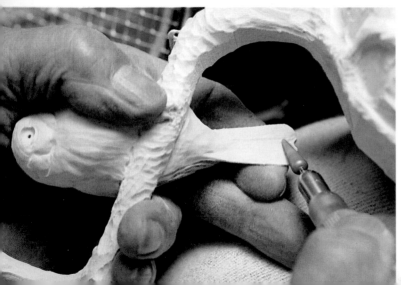

The shape of the tail is now correct. Individual feathers will be added later and the feathers will be textured.

The eyes are 5mm dark brown glass eyes. They are available from carving supply and taxidermy dealers. Ernie has already trial-fitted the eyes, and now he inserts them, using the hole drilled earlier as a guide.

Ernie pushes the wire into the hole and presses the glass eye into place with his thumb. About 1/2 inch of wire is left on the glass eye for mounting purposes. This will hold the eye in place until it can be sealed with epoxy.

The addition of the eyes makes the chickadee begin to appear lifelife. Ernie later will add epoxy eyelids to each eye.

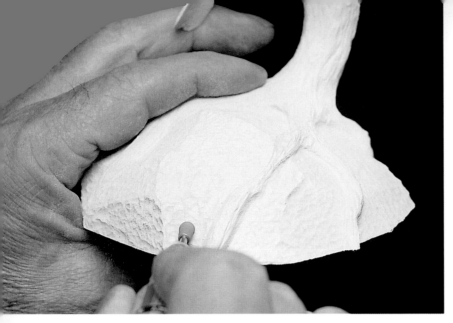

The base is an important part of the composition, and it is carved along with the bird. The roots of the weathered tree lie over a granite rock, and Ernie does the preliminary carving of this area with the stump cutter and a large diamond cutter.

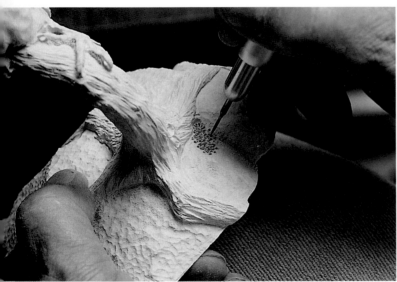

An interesting addition to the base is a patch of moss growing between two sections of root. Ernie makes moss by using a sharp needle cutter and stabbing it repeatedly into the wood.

The perforations are made at random and are very close together. The cutting tip should be held at a 90-degree angle to the surface of the wood.

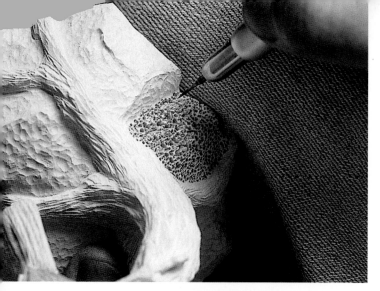

Once the area is perforated, Ernie uses the same tip to scribe horizontal lines, tearing the wood and creating a ragged appearance.

As the needle point is dragged across the perforated surface, it should be held at an angle perpendicular to the surface. The result is a texture that, when painted green, bears a remarkable resemblance to moss.

Once the moss is carved, the area is very fragile. Ernie hardens it with an application of Super Glue. He often will wait until just before painting to perform the second step of dragging the cutter through the perforated surface. This lessens the chances of damaging the moss.

Before sealing the area with Super Glue, it's important to get rid of the dust that has accumulated in the perforations. Otherwise, the glue and the dust will react to create a foam. A vacuum is handy to clean this area, but be sure not to damage the carved detail.

CHAPTER NINE

Feather Carving and Paint Preparation

The final step in the carving process is the addition of individual feathers, feather barbs, and quills where they show. Small stones mounted in the high-speed grinder are used to replicate feather detail on the small feathers and to create subtle bumps and dimples that will add to the illusion of softness. The burning pen is used to emboss feather barbs onto the large flight feathers and tail feathers.

"I try to get eighty to a hundred lines per inch with the burning pen," says Ernie. "I don't put one alongside the other in any kind of orderly progression; I just move the tip rapidly back and forth and try to get a rhythm going. I use a tight round point on the chest or other open spaces, and on wings where I have to get close to the next feather I use a spear tip. I use the Guge tip to outline feathers, like we did on the tail."

A hotter setting on the pyrographic tool is used to add feather detail to the head and chin. This darkens these areas, which will be black in the finished bird.

After the chickadee has been textured, Ernie applies Super Glue to the bill and feet to help strengthen these areas.

Preparatory to painting, he seals the surface of the wood with lacquer. On a small bird like this, he simply dips the piece into the can of lacquer instead of brushing it on. The lacquer is quickly absorbed by the wood, sealing its surface and providing a uniform painting surface.

Ernie uses two tools for carving feather detail. On small, fine feathers, such as these on the upper wing coverts, this small stone is used. Ernie has added wood filler to the area around the eye, and this will be shaped later.

Each groove left by the stone represents a feather barb or, more accurately, the space between the barbs. Ernie uses photos and other reference material to determine the direction of feather flow.

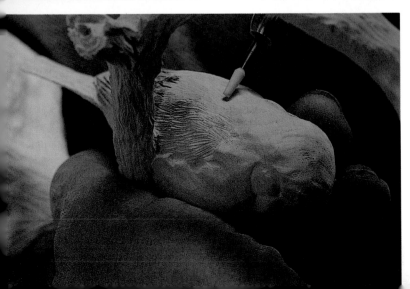

The small stone is used on the coverts and on the breast and belly, where the feathers are small and soft. Subtle bumps and dimples add to the illusion of softness.

A "defuzzer" is used to clean the filler around the eye, and Ernie burns in feather detail with the pyrographic tool. The "defuzzer" is available at carving supply dealers.

Note the bumps and subtle ridges on the breast of the chickadee. These add to the illusion of softness and should be added before texturing.

The stoned texturing is just about complete. Now Ernie will use the pyrographic tool to emboss feather barbs on the large flight feathers.

He begins with the upper, rear part of the bird, adding barbs to the tail feathers, the primaries, and the secondaries.

The spear tip point is used on the burning pen, and Ernie moves the tool rapidly back and forth, establishing a rhythm. He tries to burn eighty to one hundred lines per inch.

Note the direction of the barb lines. Good reference material is vital in achieving accuracy. Photographs, study skins, and taxidermy mounts are indispensible when carving accurate detail.

Ernie turns the heat up on his burning tool, resulting in noticeably darker feather texture on the head and bib. These areas will be dark in the finished bird, so this technique serves as a preliminary to painting.

Areas that will be white or light gray, such as the face below the eyes, are left lightly burned. Ernie calls this technique "burning for color," and he uses it extensively in his work.

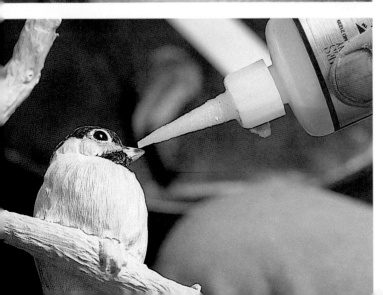

The wood is thin at the bill and feet, so these areas are subject to breakage. Ernie protects the bill with an application of Super Glue.

Super Glue is applied to the feet to add strength. Work with this material in a well-ventilated area to avoid breathing the fumes.

It is especially important to glue the areas where the toes are separated from the branch. Any fragile portion of the carving can be strengthened with Super Glue.

Prior to painting, Ernie seals the surface of the wood with lacquer. Instead of brushing it on, he simply immerses the chickadee in the can. This step is not only quicker than application with a brush, but it also ensures that the lacquer will penetrate into the finely carved detail.

Lacquer will provide a smooth, uniform painting surface and add some strength and stability to the carving. As the chickadee comes out of the can, it will dry for an hour or so and then be ready for the final step—painting.

CHAPTER TEN

Painting the Chickadee

Ernie uses acrylic tube paints, which are water soluble. For the chickadee, he will use ultramarine blue, burnt umber, raw sienna, pine green, cobalt blue, and Speedball brand warm black. Gesso will be applied first and will serve as a base for the colors. Paint adheres better to gesso than to bare wood, and the white base coat works well with the transparent washes of color that will be applied later.

He uses nylon brushes, mainly in sizes five and six. "Sable brushes are not really necessary anymore, with the quality of synthetic brushes they make now," says Ernie. "These do a good job and are inexpensive."

Ernie uses shallow trays, adding a pea-size dab of paint to about a tablespoon of water, which serves as his stockpile of color. Paint is then transferred by brush to a second tray, where one color is mixed with another.

Colors are mixed as diluted washes rather than as they come from the tube. It's easier to adjust the color that way.

Ernie paints the rock first, using a mix of ultramarine blue and burnt umber. He mixes the colors and tests the results on paper before applying it to the carving. He tries to match the color of a rock from his reference collection.

The chickadee is painted primarily in varying shades of gray and brown. Burnt umber and ultramarine blue are mixed to get the cool gray that goes on the flight feathers and tail. Burnt umber and cobalt blue produce a warmer, browner gray for the back and the tops of the upper wing coverts. Raw sienna is applied to the flanks, and Speedball warm black goes on the cap, bib, and bill.

Colors are applied as thin transparent washes, and Ernie uses a technique called blending-to-water to create soft edges where one color meets another. To do this, he applies the paint, and then with a second brush dampened with water, he softens the edge of the colored area.

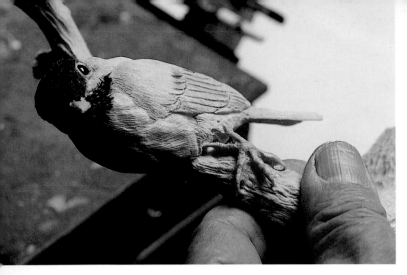

Gesso is applied as a base coat, diluted 1:1 with water. Ernie uses a dry-brush technique, dabbing excess gesso from his brush before applying it to the carving, brushing in the direction of the feather flow. It should not be applied so thickly that it obscures fine details.

Gesso is brushed on the entire bird, except for the dark cap and neck. It is lightly brushed over the moss to provide a few highlights when paint is put on later. Several coats of gesso are put on, and Ernie waits until each is dry before applying the next. The gesso should be uniform and not splotchy looking.

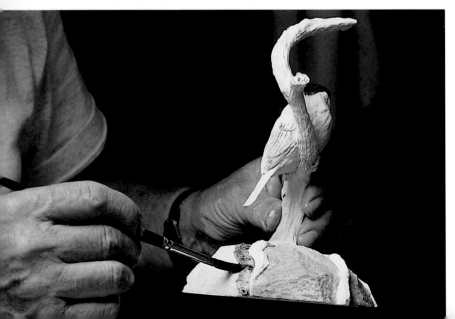

Ernie paints the rock first, using a combination of ultramarine blue and burnt umber. He tests the color on paper before applying it to the carving.

A small amount of Liquitex pearlescent medium is added to the paint to provide a rocklike sparkle. The medium has ground particles of mica in it, which produces a very natural looking rock.

Ernie applies one coat to the rock, then dabs on more paint to avoid a uniform appearance. The paint is applied thicker and darker in areas that would be shadowed. The surface also can be rubbed gently with a paper towel to create highlights.

A bit of raw sienna is dabbed onto the rock to suggest iron deposits. As with the carving process involving the rock, creativity and imagination are called for in painting.

Raw sienna, darkened with burnt umber, is applied to the flanks of the bird. Ernie uses a blending-to-water technique in which he first applies the color, and then with a second brush dampened with water, he softens the edges of the colored area.

He adds brown to the mixture applied to the rock to make a warmer gray, which goes on the branch.

The preliminary painting of the rock and branch is complete. Now Ernie is ready to paint the bird, beginning with the flight feathers and tail.

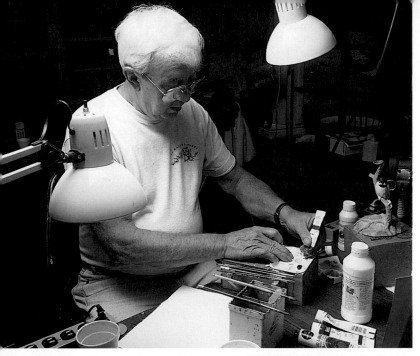

Ernie's painting area is well lighted, and he has on hand plenty of clean water, paper towels, brushes, and paints. Be sure your inventory is complete before beginning, he advises.

The paints are mixed in a shallow plastic tray that has six individual cups. He puts a pea-size dab of paint in a cup and dilutes it with a tablespoon of water.

Here, Ernie has, from left, ultramarine blue, cobalt blue, and burnt umber. The colors in these trays constitute Ernie's primary sources of color. They are diluted and then mixed with other colors to get a variety of shades.

Burnt umber and ultramarine blue are diluted with water and then mixed to get the desired shades of gray that will go on the primary, secondary, and tail feathers.

The wings are also painted with a mixture of ultramarine blue and burnt umber. Ernie mixes the two colors in a cup and tests the color on a piece of paper. More blue produces a cooler gray; more burnt umber a warmer gray.

Ernie paints the wing feathers, leaving a light trailing edge, which is appropriate with the black-capped chickadee. If you are carving a Carolina chickadee, omit the white trailing edges.

He applies several washes of this color. The inner portions of the feathers are darker, so Ernie concentrates the color in this area. It's important to have good reference material, such as photographs and study skins, when doing this.

The tail feathers are painted with the same color, using the same technique, leaving a light edge. The colors are applied in thin, diluted washes and are built up gradually.

A small brush that "points up" well is necessary when painting fine detail such as this. Ernie uses nylon brushes, mainly in sizes 5 and 6, but smaller for adding fine detail.

The inner edges of the feathers are darkened by applying additional washes. The same color is used, but the addition of more pigment causes the inner edges to darken.

The same thing is done on the right side of the bird. Multiple thin washes are used to build up color through transparent washes, with more applications on the inner edges of the feathers.

Additional washes are also applied to the inner portions of the tail feathers. As with the wing features, this step gradually darkens the inner parts of these feathers.

The edges of the coverts and secondaries are shadowed slightly with the mix of burnt umber and ultramarine blue.

With the flight feathers and tail painted, Ernie applies a thin wash of the same color over the entire area. This makes the effect more subtle, bringing the values of the inner feather and feather edge closer together.

The same color is applied to the leg and foot. Again, multiple thin washes are applied and are dried between coats with a portable hair dryer.

Cobalt blue and burnt umber are mixed for painting the back and the tops of the upper wing coverts. This produces a slightly warmer, browner gray than the ultramarine blue and burnt umber combination used on the flight feathers.

Ernie uses the blend-to-water technique again to avoid getting hard edges where the colors meet. He first applies color, then uses a second brush dampened with water to soften the edge.

The color is built up through a succession of thin washes. Ernie will put on four coats. "It's better to err on the side of having the wash too thin than too thick," he says.

Speedball brand warm black, diluted with water, is put on the head. The dark, burned surface makes the process of building up color easier.

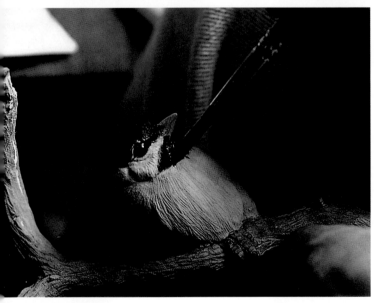

Speedball warm black also goes on the bib. This is a rich, deep black that complements the burned detail.

For the bill, Ernie mixes equal parts matte medium and water, and then adds warm black. Multiple diluted applications are made until the bill slowly becomes black. The matte medium and the repeated applications produce a leathery look. The same solution is put on the toenails.

The final step is to apply Jo Sonja's pine green to the moss and along the edges of the roots. An earlier light application of gesso helps create subtle highlights.

The paint is worked down into the perforations with the brush to cover all unpainted areas. Super Glue helps strengthen this fragile detail, making painting easier.

Pages 87 through 92 show the completed carving.